The Authentic Connection: Nurturing Lasting Relationships with Women

Maxwell Hartley

Published by Serene Publishing House, 2023.

THE AUTHENTIC CONNECTION: NURTURING LASTING RELATIONSHIPS WITH WOMEN

First edition. July 9, 2023.

Copyright © 2023 Maxwell Hartley.

ISBN: 979-8223103554

Written by Maxwell Hartley.

Chapter 1: Understanding Authenticity and its Role in Relationships

Section 1: What is authenticity?

Authenticity is the quality of being true to oneself and genuinely expressing one's thoughts, feelings, and values. It involves aligning your actions, words, and beliefs, without pretense or the need to conform to external expectations. Authenticity is about embracing your uniqueness and embracing your true self, rather than trying to portray an image that you believe others want to see.

Subsection 1.1: The Essence of Authenticity

Authenticity goes beyond superficial appearances and societal norms. It is about embracing your strengths and weaknesses, acknowledging your true emotions, and expressing yourself honestly. It requires self-awareness and the courage to be vulnerable, allowing others to see the real you.

Subsection 1.2: Recognizing Inauthenticity

To understand authenticity, it is essential to recognize signs of inauthenticity. This includes behaviors such as people-pleasing, hiding true emotions, pretending to be someone you're not, or engaging in deceptive practices to gain acceptance or approval. Inauthenticity often leads to shallow connections and a lack of fulfillment in relationships.

Subsection 1.3: The Impact of Authenticity in Relationships

Authenticity plays a vital role in building lasting relationships. When you are authentic, you create an environment of trust and openness. Authenticity allows you to connect on a deeper level, as it fosters genuine understanding, empathy, and emotional intimacy. It enables you to form meaningful connections with women based on mutual respect and appreciation for each other's true selves.

Subsection 1.4: Benefits of Embracing Authenticity

Embracing authenticity brings numerous benefits to both yourself and your relationships. It enhances self-confidence and self-acceptance, enabling you to attract partners who appreciate you for who you truly are. Authenticity also promotes healthier communication, conflict resolution, and the ability to navigate challenges with honesty and integrity.

Section 2: The Impact of Authenticity on Relationship Quality

Authenticity has a profound impact on the quality of relationships, particularly when it comes to forming lasting connections with women. When both individuals in a relationship are authentic, it sets the stage for a strong and meaningful bond. Here are some key ways in which authenticity influences relationship quality:

Subsection 2.1: Building Trust and Emotional Safety

Authenticity builds trust and creates a safe emotional space within a relationship. When you are authentic, you show your true self, including your vulnerabilities and insecurities. This openness fosters trust because it demonstrates that you are genuine and reliable. It encourages your partner to reciprocate by also being open and vulnerable, leading to a deeper emotional connection.

Subsection 2.2: Enhanced Communication and Understanding

Authenticity promotes open and honest communication, which is vital for healthy relationships. When you express yourself authentically, you convey your true thoughts, emotions, and needs. This level of openness allows for genuine understanding between partners. Authenticity in communication helps avoid misunderstandings, facilitates problem-solving, and creates an environment where both partners feel heard and valued.

Subsection 2.3: Strengthening Emotional Intimacy

Authenticity paves the way for deeper emotional intimacy. By being authentic, you share your true emotions and experiences with your partner, allowing for a deeper connection. This emotional vulnerability allows both partners to connect on a more profound level, fostering empathy, compassion, and a sense of closeness.

Subsection 2.4: Mutual Respect and Acceptance

When authenticity is present in a relationship, both partners can be themselves without fear of judgment or rejection. This mutual acceptance and respect for each other's authentic selves create a supportive and nurturing dynamic. Authenticity allows partners to appreciate and embrace each other's unique qualities, fostering a deeper sense of love and connection.

Subsection 2.5: Long-Term Relationship Satisfaction

Authenticity contributes to long-term relationship satisfaction. When both partners are authentic, it creates a solid foundation of trust, effective communication, emotional intimacy, and mutual respect. These elements are crucial for maintaining a healthy and fulfilling relationship over time, as they foster growth, support, and the ability to navigate challenges together.

Section 3: The Benefits of Being True to Yourself

Being true to yourself and embracing authenticity brings about numerous benefits, not only in relationships with women but also in your overall well-being. Here are some key benefits of being true to yourself:

Subsection 3.1: Self-Confidence and Self-Acceptance

Embracing authenticity fosters self-confidence and self-acceptance. When you are true to yourself, you no longer feel the need to conform to societal expectations or pretend to be someone you're not. This self-assurance radiates in your interactions with others, including women, as you embrace your unique qualities, strengths, and values.

Subsection 3.2: Attracting the Right Partners

Being authentic helps attract partners who appreciate you for who you truly are. When you are genuine and authentic, you naturally attract individuals who resonate with your authentic self. By being true to yourself, you can form relationships with women who value and connect with the real you, leading to more fulfilling and compatible partnerships.

Subsection 3.3: Improved Communication and Conflict Resolution

Authenticity enhances your communication skills and conflict resolution abilities. When you are true to yourself, you are better able to express your thoughts, emotions, and needs honestly and effectively. This clarity in communication fosters understanding and enables you to address conflicts in a healthy and productive manner, leading to stronger and more harmonious relationships.

Subsection 3.4: Emotional Well-being and Inner Alignment

Being true to yourself promotes emotional well-being and inner alignment. When you embrace authenticity, you experience a sense of congruence between your inner self and outward expressions. This alignment brings a deep sense of fulfillment and contentment, positively impacting your overall happiness and mental well-being.

Subsection 3.5: Freedom from Pretense and Expectations

By being true to yourself, you free yourself from the burden of pretense and societal expectations. Authenticity allows you to break free from the pressure to conform, enabling you to live a life that aligns with your true values, aspirations, and passions. This freedom cultivates a sense of liberation, allowing you to build relationships and pursue experiences that resonate with your authentic self.

Chapter 2: Self-Reflection and Authenticity

Section 1: Exploring your values and beliefs

Understanding your values and beliefs is a crucial step in embracing authenticity and building lasting relationships with women. By exploring and clarifying your own values and beliefs, you lay the groundwork for living a life that aligns with your authentic self. Here are some key aspects to consider:

Subsection 1.1: The Importance of Values and Beliefs

Values and beliefs serve as guiding principles that shape our thoughts, actions, and decisions. They reflect what we consider important, meaningful, and true. Identifying and understanding your values and beliefs is essential because they form the core of your authentic self.

Subsection 1.2: Reflecting on Personal Values

Take time to reflect on your personal values. What qualities and principles do you hold dear? Consider areas such as integrity, compassion, honesty, respect, growth, family, career, spirituality, or social justice. Reflect on experiences and moments in your life that have shaped and influenced your values.

Subsection 1.3: Exploring Core Beliefs

Examine your core beliefs, which are deeply ingrained assumptions and perspectives that influence your thoughts and actions. These beliefs may revolve around relationships, gender roles, self-worth, or other aspects of life. Reflect on where these beliefs originated and whether they align with your authentic self or if they require reevaluation.

Subsection 1.4: Identifying Non-negotiables

Non-negotiables are values or beliefs that you consider essential in a relationship. These are boundaries that you won't compromise on. Reflect on what qualities, behaviors, or values are non-negotiable for you in a partner. Understanding these non-negotiables helps you make conscious choices and build relationships that align with your authenticity.

Subsection 1.5: Alignment with Your Authentic Self

Assess whether your current lifestyle, choices, and relationships align with your values and beliefs. Identify areas where there might be incongruence. Reflect on how aligning your actions and choices with your authentic self can enhance your relationships with women and contribute to your overall fulfillment.

Section 2: Embracing your strengths and weaknesses

Embracing your strengths and weaknesses is an integral part of embracing authenticity. Recognizing and accepting both your positive qualities and areas for growth allows you to present your true self to others and build genuine connections. Here are key aspects to consider when embracing your strengths and weaknesses:

Subsection 2.1: Identifying Your Strengths

Take time to identify and acknowledge your strengths. These are the qualities, skills, or attributes that come naturally to you and contribute to your personal growth and success. Reflect on your achievements, positive feedback you've received, and activities that bring you joy and fulfillment. Embracing and showcasing your strengths helps you build confidence and authenticity in your interactions with women.

Subsection 2.2: Owning Your Weaknesses

Recognize and accept your weaknesses as areas for growth and improvement. We all have areas where we may struggle or have limitations. Embrace the opportunity to learn and develop in these areas rather than hiding or denying them. Acknowledging your weaknesses demonstrates self-awareness and authenticity, allowing you to approach relationships with humility and openness.

Subsection 2.3: Emphasizing Authenticity over Perfection

Shift your focus from striving for perfection to embracing authenticity. Perfectionism can hinder genuine connections, as it often involves projecting an image of flawlessness or fear of being vulnerable. Embrace the beauty of your imperfections and recognize that being authentic means being true to yourself, strengths, weaknesses, and all.

Subsection 2.4: Honoring Individuality and Uniqueness

Appreciate and celebrate your unique qualities and individuality. Each person has a distinctive combination of strengths and weaknesses. Embracing your uniqueness allows you to bring something special to your relationships with women. It sets you apart and can be attractive to others who appreciate your genuine self.

Subsection 2.5: Cultivating Self-Improvement

While embracing your strengths and weaknesses, also strive for personal growth and development. Seek opportunities to enhance your strengths further and work on areas where you'd like to improve. Cultivating self-improvement demonstrates a commitment to personal growth and authenticity, allowing you to continuously evolve and build meaningful connections.

Section 3: Overcoming insecurities and fears

Overcoming insecurities and fears is an essential part of embracing authenticity and building lasting relationships with women. Insecurities and fears can hinder your ability to connect genuinely and hinder your personal growth. Here are key aspects to consider when overcoming insecurities and fears:

Subsection 3.1: Identifying Insecurities

Take a courageous look at your insecurities. These are the doubts or negative beliefs you hold about yourself. Reflect on the areas where you feel inadequate, self-conscious, or fearful. Identifying your insecurities is the first step in understanding and addressing them.

Subsection 3.2: Challenging Negative Self-Talk

Recognize that negative self-talk contributes to insecurities and fears. Challenge the negative thoughts and beliefs that undermine your confidence and authenticity. Replace them with positive and affirming thoughts that align with your true worth and potential.

Subsection 3.3: Seeking Support and Encouragement

Reach out to supportive friends, mentors, or professionals who can provide guidance and encouragement. Share your insecurities and fears with trusted individuals who can offer valuable perspectives, advice, and emotional support. Surrounding yourself with a positive support system can help you overcome insecurities and build self-confidence.

Subsection 3.4: Confronting and Embracing Vulnerability

Embrace vulnerability as a pathway to authenticity. Recognize that everyone experiences vulnerability, and it is a natural part of building relationships. Take small steps towards vulnerability by opening up and expressing your thoughts, feelings, and fears with others, including women you trust. Embracing vulnerability fosters connection and deepens relationships.

Subsection 3.5: Challenging Fear of Rejection

Fear of rejection can hold you back from authentic connections. Challenge this fear by recognizing that rejection is a part of life and does not define your worth. Focus on self-acceptance and resilience, knowing that genuine connections require vulnerability and taking risks.

Subsection 3.6: Setting Realistic Expectations

Set realistic expectations for yourself and relationships. Avoid comparing yourself to others or holding unrealistic standards. Embrace the journey of personal growth and understand that building lasting connections takes time, patience, and effort.

Chapter 3: Active Listening: The Foundation of Authentic Connection

Section 1: The Power of Active Listening in Building Connections

Active listening is a fundamental skill that plays a pivotal role in building authentic connections with women. It involves fully engaging in the process of listening, not only to the words being spoken but also to the underlying emotions and messages being conveyed. Here are key aspects to consider regarding the power of active listening in building connections:

Subsection 1.1: Creating a Safe and Supportive Environment

Active listening creates a safe and supportive environment for open and honest communication. By giving your undivided attention and showing genuine interest in what the other person is saying, you signal that their thoughts and feelings are valued. This fosters trust, allowing women to feel comfortable and encouraged to share their authentic selves.

Subsection 1.2: Enhancing Understanding and Empathy

Active listening promotes understanding and empathy. When you actively listen, you strive to comprehend not only the words but also the emotions and perspectives behind them. By listening empathetically, you demonstrate a genuine desire to understand the experiences and feelings of the women you interact with. This fosters a deeper sense of connection and emotional intimacy.

Subsection 1.3: Validating and Affirming Experiences

Active listening validates and affirms the experiences of women. By actively engaging in listening, you acknowledge and validate their emotions, thoughts, and experiences without judgment. This validation creates a sense of acceptance and appreciation, fostering an authentic connection based on mutual respect and understanding.

Subsection 1.4: Building Trust and Strengthening Relationships

Active listening is instrumental in building trust and strengthening relationships. When women feel genuinely heard and understood, they develop trust in your intentions and authenticity. This trust forms the foundation for deeper connections, allowing relationships to flourish and thrive.

Subsection 1.5: Fostering Effective Problem-Solving and Conflict Resolution

Active listening is vital for effective problem-solving and conflict resolution. By attentively listening to the concerns, perspectives, and needs of women, you gain a comprehensive understanding of the situation. This understanding enables you to collaborate in finding mutually beneficial solutions and navigate conflicts with empathy and respect, reinforcing the authenticity of the connection.

Subsection 1.6: Cultivating Presence and Mindfulness

Active listening cultivates presence and mindfulness in your interactions. By consciously focusing on the present moment and suspending judgment or preconceived notions, you create space for deeper connections to unfold. This presence allows you to connect authentically with women, fostering meaningful and genuine relationships.

Section 2: Developing Listening Skills and Techniques

Developing effective listening skills and techniques is essential to becoming a proficient active listener. These skills enable you to fully engage in conversations, understand others' perspectives, and build authentic connections. Here are key aspects to consider when developing listening skills and techniques:

Subsection 2.1: Practice Mindful Presence

Cultivate mindful presence by focusing your attention fully on the speaker and the present moment. Avoid distractions and be fully engaged in the conversation. This allows you to pick up on verbal and non-verbal cues and enhances your ability to actively listen.

Subsection 2.2: Maintain Eye Contact

Maintain appropriate eye contact to demonstrate your attentiveness and interest in the speaker. Eye contact signals that you are fully present and engaged, which encourages open and authentic communication.

Subsection 2.3: Use Verbal and Non-Verbal Cues

Use verbal cues such as nodding, affirming statements, and encouraging words to show that you are actively listening and acknowledging what the speaker is saying. Additionally, non-verbal cues like facial expressions, posture, and gestures can convey your attentiveness and understanding.

Subsection 2.4: Reflect and Paraphrase

Practice reflection and paraphrasing to ensure accurate understanding. Reflecting involves summarizing the speaker's main points and feelings, while paraphrasing involves restating their ideas in your own words. This technique shows that you are actively processing the information and seeking clarity.

Subsection 2.5: Ask Open-Ended Questions

Ask open-ended questions to encourage further elaboration and exploration of the speaker's thoughts and feelings. Open-ended questions promote meaningful conversations and provide opportunities for deeper connection and understanding.

Subsection 2.6: Avoid Interrupting or Jumping to Solutions

Resist the urge to interrupt or jump to solutions prematurely. Allow the speaker to express themselves fully before offering your perspective or advice. This demonstrates respect for their autonomy and shows that you value their voice and experiences.

Subsection 2.7: Cultivate Empathy and Non-Judgment

Approach conversations with empathy and non-judgment. Seek to understand the speaker's perspective without imposing your own biases or preconceptions. This creates a safe space for open and authentic expression, fostering trust and connection.

Subsection 2.8: Practice Active Listening in Daily Interactions

Extend your active listening practice to your daily interactions. Engage fully in conversations with friends, family, and colleagues. By consistently practicing active listening, you can develop it into a natural and effortless skill.

Section 3: Non-verbal cues and their significance in communication

Non-verbal cues play a significant role in communication, complementing verbal messages and conveying emotions, attitudes, and intentions. Being attuned to non-verbal cues enhances your active listening skills and helps you build authentic connections. Here are key aspects to consider regarding non-verbal cues and their significance in communication:

Subsection 3.1: Body Language

Pay attention to body language, which includes gestures, facial expressions, posture, and eye contact. Body language can provide valuable insights into a person's emotions, level of engagement, and comfort. For example, crossed arms may indicate defensiveness or closed-off feelings, while open and relaxed postures reflect a more receptive attitude.

Subsection 3.2: Facial Expressions

Facial expressions convey a wealth of emotions and can help you understand the speaker's feelings beyond their words. Smiles, frowns, raised eyebrows, or furrowed brows can indicate happiness, confusion, surprise, or concern. Observing facial expressions in conjunction with verbal messages deepens your comprehension of the speaker's underlying emotions.

Subsection 3.3: Eye Contact

Eye contact is a powerful non-verbal cue that signals engagement and interest. Sustained eye contact demonstrates active listening and respect for the speaker. It fosters a sense of connection and trust. However, cultural norms and individual preferences can influence eye contact levels, so be mindful of these variations.

Subsection 3.4: Tone of Voice

The tone of voice conveys emotions, attitudes, and meaning. Pay attention to variations in pitch, volume, and pace. A warm and enthusiastic tone suggests interest and engagement, while a flat or harsh tone may indicate disinterest or frustration. Combined with verbal content, tone of voice provides crucial insights into the speaker's emotions and intentions.

Subsection 3.5: Proxemics and Personal Space

Proxemics refers to the use of personal space during communication. Respect personal boundaries and adapt your proximity accordingly. Invading personal space may make the speaker uncomfortable, while maintaining an appropriate distance signals respect and consideration.

Subsection 3.6: Microexpressions

Microexpressions are brief and subtle facial expressions that flash across a person's face, often revealing their true emotions. These fleeting expressions can provide valuable cues about underlying feelings or reactions that may not be explicitly expressed in words. Paying attention to microexpressions helps you discern the speaker's true sentiments.

Subsection 3.7: Congruence and Incongruence

Non-verbal cues should align with the speaker's verbal messages to establish authenticity and trust. Incongruence occurs when there is a mismatch between verbal and non-verbal cues. Being aware of incongruence helps you navigate potential miscommunication and address discrepancies with sensitivity and curiosity.

Chapter 4: Expressing Vulnerability: Opening Up and Creating Trust

Section 1: The Role of Vulnerability in Building Trust

Vulnerability plays a crucial role in building trust and fostering authentic connections. When you allow yourself to be vulnerable, you create an environment of openness and emotional honesty. Here are key aspects to consider regarding the role of vulnerability in building trust:

Subsection 1.1: Authenticity and Genuine Connection

Vulnerability allows you to show your authentic self to others. By expressing vulnerability, you demonstrate that you are willing to be honest and transparent, which fosters genuine connections. This authenticity builds trust, as others perceive that you are not hiding behind a façade.

Subsection 1.2: Building Emotional Intimacy

Expressing vulnerability opens the door to emotional intimacy. When you share your fears, insecurities, and personal struggles with someone, it deepens the level of emotional connection and understanding. This vulnerability cultivates a safe space where both parties can be open and supported.

Subsection 1.3: Mutual Sharing and Empathy

When you express vulnerability, it often encourages others to do the same. By sharing your own experiences and emotions, you create a safe and accepting space for others to share their vulnerabilities. This mutual exchange of vulnerability fosters empathy and understanding, strengthening the bond of trust.

Subsection 1.4: Overcoming Fear and Judgment

Vulnerability requires courage, as it involves the risk of being judged or rejected. However, by taking that risk, you give others the opportunity to see your true self and demonstrate acceptance. When you overcome the fear of judgment and embrace vulnerability, it paves the way for deeper trust and connection.

Subsection 1.5: Strengthening Emotional Resilience

Expressing vulnerability and receiving support builds emotional resilience. Sharing your vulnerabilities with others and being met with understanding and empathy reinforces your ability to cope with challenges and bounce back from difficult situations. This resilience enhances your overall well-being and strengthens the trust in your relationships.

Subsection 1.6: Honoring Boundaries and Consent

It is important to note that vulnerability should be shared within appropriate boundaries and with consent. Respecting the boundaries and comfort levels of both yourself and the other person is crucial in building trust. It is a collaborative process that requires ongoing communication and consent.

Section 2: Overcoming the Fear of Vulnerability

Overcoming the fear of vulnerability is a transformative process that allows you to build deeper connections with others. By addressing and working through this fear, you can cultivate authentic relationships based on trust and emotional intimacy. Here are key aspects to consider when overcoming the fear of vulnerability:

Subsection 2.1: Recognizing the Fear

Begin by acknowledging and recognizing your fear of vulnerability. Understand that it is a common and natural fear that many people experience. By acknowledging this fear, you can start to confront it and explore its underlying causes.

Subsection 2.2: Understanding the Benefits of Vulnerability

Shift your perspective by focusing on the potential benefits of vulnerability. Recognize that by allowing yourself to be vulnerable, you create opportunities for deeper connections, emotional growth, and increased authenticity in your relationships. Emphasize the positive outcomes that can arise from taking this courageous step.

Subsection 2.3: Reflecting on Past Experiences

Reflect on past experiences where vulnerability has led to positive outcomes. Recall moments when you took emotional risks and were met with understanding, acceptance, and support. Reminding yourself of these instances can help counterbalance negative expectations and build confidence in your ability to handle vulnerability.

Subsection 2.4: Challenging Limiting Beliefs

Identify and challenge any limiting beliefs or negative self-talk surrounding vulnerability. Explore the thoughts and assumptions that fuel your fear, and consciously challenge them with more realistic and empowering perspectives. Replace self-doubt with self-compassion and affirmations that reinforce your worthiness of connection and support.

Subsection 2.5: Gradual Exposure to Vulnerability

Ease into vulnerability by taking small, calculated steps. Start by sharing thoughts or feelings with someone you trust and feel comfortable with. Gradually increase the depth of your vulnerability as you build trust and confidence. Each small step builds resilience and reinforces the understanding that vulnerability can be met with understanding and support.

Subsection 2.6: Building a Supportive Network

Surround yourself with a supportive network of friends, family, or a therapist who can offer guidance and encouragement. Seek out individuals who validate your experiences and provide a safe space for vulnerability. Having a supportive network helps alleviate the fear and provides a solid foundation for taking emotional risks.

Subsection 2.7: Practicing Self-Compassion

Be kind and patient with yourself throughout the process of overcoming the fear of vulnerability. Practice self-compassion by recognizing that vulnerability requires courage and that it is okay to feel vulnerable. Embrace self-care practices that nurture your emotional well-being and reinforce your resilience.

Section 3: Creating a Safe Space for Open and Honest Communication

Creating a safe space for open and honest communication is essential for fostering vulnerability, trust, and authentic connections. When individuals feel secure and accepted, they are more likely to share their thoughts, feelings, and vulnerabilities. Here are key aspects to consider when creating a safe space for open and honest communication:

Subsection 3.1: Cultivating Active Listening

Practice active listening, as discussed in Chapter 3, to demonstrate your attentiveness and genuine interest in what the other person is saying. By giving your undivided attention and suspending judgment, you create an environment where individuals feel heard, understood, and valued. Active listening encourages open and honest communication.

Subsection 3.2: Practicing Empathy and Understanding

Approach conversations with empathy and a genuine desire to understand the other person's perspective. Seek to put yourself in their shoes and validate their emotions and experiences. Show empathy through verbal and non-verbal cues, allowing individuals to feel safe and supported in expressing their authentic selves.

Subsection 3.3: Promoting Non-Judgmental Attitudes

Create an atmosphere of non-judgment, where individuals feel free to express themselves without fear of criticism or ridicule. Encourage open-mindedness and respect for diverse opinions and experiences. By fostering a non-judgmental environment, you create space for authentic conversations and encourage others to share openly.

Subsection 3.4: Honoring Confidentiality and Trust

Respect the confidentiality of shared information and maintain trust. Assure individuals that what they share with you will be kept in confidence unless there are concerns for their safety or the safety of others. Building trust through confidentiality allows individuals to feel secure in opening up and sharing their vulnerabilities.

Subsection 3.5: Emphasizing Emotional Safety

Emphasize emotional safety by creating an environment where individuals feel emotionally secure and comfortable. Foster an atmosphere of acceptance, understanding, and support. Encourage emotional expression without judgment or shaming. Emotional safety allows individuals to share their authentic selves openly and honestly.

Subsection 3.6: Encouraging Open Dialogue and Feedback

Promote open dialogue and encourage individuals to express their thoughts, concerns, and feelings. Create space for constructive feedback and ensure that everyone's voice is heard and valued. By fostering open communication, you create an environment where everyone can contribute authentically and feel respected.

Subsection 3.7: Building Trust Through Consistency

Consistency in your actions and words is crucial for building trust and creating a safe space. Be reliable, follow through on commitments, and demonstrate integrity in your interactions. Consistency reinforces the belief that your intentions are genuine and that the safe space you create is reliable and trustworthy.

Chapter 5: Genuine Empathy: Understanding and Respecting Her Perspective

Section 1: Developing Empathy and Emotional Intelligence

Developing empathy and emotional intelligence is essential for understanding and respecting a woman's perspective. These qualities enable you to connect on a deeper level, empathize with her experiences, and build authentic connections. Here are key aspects to consider when developing empathy and emotional intelligence:

Subsection 1.1: Cultivating Self-Awareness

Begin by cultivating self-awareness, which involves understanding your own emotions, thoughts, and reactions. By being aware of your own emotional landscape, you can better understand and empathize with the emotions of others. Practice mindfulness and self-reflection to enhance your self-awareness.

Subsection 1.2: Practicing Perspective-Taking

Practice perspective-taking, which involves putting yourself in another person's shoes and trying to understand their thoughts, feelings, and experiences. Imagine how you would feel and react in a similar situation. This exercise helps you develop empathy and gain insight into a woman's perspective.

Subsection 1.3: Active Listening and Validation

Engage in active listening, as discussed in Chapter 3, to genuinely understand and validate a woman's perspective. Show empathy by reflecting her feelings and experiences. Validate her emotions by acknowledging and accepting them without judgment. This demonstrates that you respect and value her perspective.

Subsection 1.4: Emotional Regulation

Develop emotional regulation skills to manage your own emotions effectively. This allows you to be present and empathetic without being overwhelmed or reactive. By regulating your own emotions, you create a space for genuine empathy and connection with a woman's experiences.

Subsection 1.5: Cultural Sensitivity

Be aware of and sensitive to cultural differences and diverse backgrounds. Recognize that different individuals may have unique experiences and perspectives shaped by their cultural and social contexts. Educate yourself and engage in open-minded conversations to enhance your cultural sensitivity and understanding.

Subsection 1.6: Empathetic Communication

Practice empathetic communication by expressing understanding, concern, and support in your conversations with women. Use phrases such as "I can imagine that must have been challenging" or "I understand why you feel that way." This type of communication conveys empathy and helps foster a deeper connection.

Subsection 1.7: Developing Emotional Intelligence

Develop overall emotional intelligence, which includes self-awareness, self-regulation, empathy, social skills, and motivation. Strengthening emotional intelligence enables you to navigate and respond effectively to emotional cues and to connect authentically with others, including women.

Subsection 1.8: Practicing Empathy in Daily Interactions

Extend your practice of empathy beyond specific interactions with women and apply it to your daily interactions with people. Seek opportunities to empathize with others' perspectives, feelings, and experiences. By incorporating empathy into your daily life, it becomes a natural and integral part of your interactions.

Section 2: Active Empathy: Putting Yourself in Her Shoes

Active empathy involves actively imagining yourself in a woman's position, understanding her emotions, and considering her experiences from her perspective. By putting yourself in her shoes, you can deepen your understanding, foster connection, and build authentic relationships. Here are key aspects to consider when practicing active empathy:

Subsection 2.1: Cultivating Curiosity and Openness

Approach interactions with a genuine curiosity and open-mindedness. Be receptive to learning about a woman's experiences, thoughts, and emotions. Allow yourself to suspend judgment and truly engage in understanding her perspective.

Subsection 2.2: Listening with Empathy

Engage in active listening and make a conscious effort to listen with empathy. Pay attention not only to the words being spoken but also to the emotions, body language, and underlying messages being conveyed. Seek to understand the emotions behind her words and validate her experiences.

Subsection 2.3: Imagining the Emotional Impact

Put yourself in her shoes by imagining how the situation might be affecting her emotionally. Consider her feelings, concerns, and vulnerabilities. Reflect on how you would feel if you were in her position.

This exercise helps you develop a deeper sense of empathy and understanding.

Subsection 2.4: Reflecting on Similar Experiences

Reflect on similar experiences you may have had and how they made you feel. Draw upon these experiences to better relate to and empathize with her emotions and reactions. Find common ground and use it as a basis for connecting and supporting her.

Subsection 2.5: Asking Empathetic Questions

Ask open-ended, empathetic questions that encourage her to share her perspective and feelings. This demonstrates your genuine interest in understanding her experiences. Ask questions that delve deeper into her emotions, motivations, and reactions to gain a more comprehensive understanding.

Subsection 2.6: Validating and Affirming Her Feelings

Validate and affirm her feelings by acknowledging and accepting them without judgment. Express empathy and understanding, letting her know that her emotions are valid and heard. This validation creates a safe space for her to open up and share more authentically.

Subsection 2.7: Practicing Empathy in Action

Go beyond understanding and actively practice empathy in your actions. Consider what actions or support she might need based on her perspective and emotions. Show up for her in a way that demonstrates your empathy and willingness to be there for her.

Subsection 2.8: Reflecting and Learning from the Experience

Take time to reflect on the insights gained from putting yourself in her shoes. Consider how this understanding can shape your future interactions and relationships. Learn from the experience and use it to continuously grow your capacity for empathy.

Section 3: Respecting Her Emotions and Experiences

Respecting a woman's emotions and experiences is crucial for building trust, fostering connection, and maintaining authentic relationships. It involves recognizing the validity of her feelings, honoring her unique experiences, and treating her with empathy and sensitivity. Here are key aspects to consider when respecting her emotions and experiences:

Subsection 3.1: Validating Her Emotions

Validate her emotions by acknowledging and accepting them without judgment. Understand that her emotions are real and important, even if they differ from your own. Let her know that you appreciate her sharing her feelings and that you are there to support her.

Subsection 3.2: Listening with Empathy and Understanding

Listen actively and empathetically to her experiences and perspectives. Be present and attentive, giving her your full focus. Seek to understand her point of view and avoid dismissing or minimizing her emotions. Show genuine empathy and understanding in your responses.

Subsection 3.3: Avoiding Judgment and Criticism

Refrain from judging or criticizing her emotions or experiences. Understand that everyone has their own unique journey and valid responses to situations. Avoid making assumptions or belittling her feelings. Instead, offer a safe space where she feels respected and accepted.

Subsection 3.4: Honoring Her Autonomy

Respect her autonomy by allowing her to express her emotions and make her own choices. Avoid pressuring her to feel or react a certain way. Recognize that she has agency over her own emotions and experiences, and offer support and understanding as she navigates them.

Subsection 3.5: Practicing Empathetic Communication

Communicate with empathy, using language that reflects your respect for her emotions and experiences. Use phrases like "I understand how that could be challenging for you" or "It's understandable that you would feel that way." Express empathy and validate her feelings through your words.

Subsection 3.6: Empowering Her Voice

Encourage her to share her emotions and experiences openly and honestly. Create an environment where she feels safe and supported in expressing herself. Validate her perspectives and give her space to voice her thoughts and feelings. Empower her to own and express her emotions.

Subsection 3.7: Offering Support and Understanding

Provide support and understanding as she navigates her emotions and experiences. Be there to listen, offer a shoulder to lean on, or provide practical assistance when needed. Show empathy and compassion, demonstrating your commitment to being there for her.

Subsection 3.8: Respecting Boundaries

Respect her boundaries when it comes to discussing emotions and experiences. Understand that not all topics may be comfortable for her to discuss openly, and that's okay. Be attentive to cues and signals, and be respectful if she prefers to maintain privacy or needs space.

Chapter 6: Authentic Communication: Honesty, Transparency, and Boundaries

Section 1: The Importance of Honesty in Relationships

Honesty forms the bedrock of authentic communication and is vital for building and maintaining healthy relationships. It involves being truthful, sincere, and transparent in your interactions with women. Here are key aspects to consider regarding the importance of honesty in relationships:

Subsection 1.1: Building Trust

Honesty is essential for building trust. When you consistently communicate truthfully and transparently, women can rely on your words and actions. They feel secure knowing that they can trust you to be honest, which fosters a foundation of trust in the relationship.

Subsection 1.2: Establishing Authenticity

Honesty allows you to establish authenticity in your interactions. By being honest, you present your true self to women, without pretense or masks. This authenticity paves the way for genuine connections based on mutual understanding and acceptance.

Subsection 1.3: Enhancing Emotional Intimacy

Honesty nurtures emotional intimacy. When you share your thoughts, feelings, and experiences openly and honestly, you invite women to do the same. This vulnerability deepens the emotional connection, fostering intimacy and closeness in the relationship.

Subsection 1.4: Resolving Conflicts Effectively

Honesty is crucial for resolving conflicts in a healthy and constructive manner. By openly expressing your concerns, needs, and boundaries, you create an environment where conflicts can be addressed and resolved through open dialogue. Honesty allows for a deeper understanding of each other's perspectives, leading to effective conflict resolution.

Subsection 1.5: Maintaining Respect and Integrity

Honesty is a testament to your respect for others and your own integrity. By being honest, you show respect for women by valuing their right to know the truth and make informed decisions. Moreover, honesty demonstrates your personal integrity, highlighting your commitment to ethical and transparent communication.

Subsection 1.6: Fostering Emotional Safety

Honesty contributes to emotional safety in relationships. When you are honest, women feel secure knowing that you are reliable and forthcoming. They can express themselves without fear of deception or hidden agendas. This emotional safety nurtures trust and allows for deeper emotional connection.

Subsection 1.7: Nurturing Long-Term Relationships

Honesty is key to nurturing long-term relationships. By consistently being honest, you establish a foundation of trust, authenticity, and open communication. This fosters a sense of security and stability, contributing to the growth and longevity of the relationship.

Subsection 1.8: Honesty with Yourself

Remember that honesty starts with being honest with yourself. Reflect on your own thoughts, feelings, and motivations. Practice self-awareness and self-honesty, as this sets the tone for honest communication with others.

Section 2: Communicating Your Needs and Desires Effectively

Communicating your needs and desires effectively is crucial for fostering understanding, mutual satisfaction, and healthy relationships with women. By expressing yourself clearly and assertively, you create an environment where your needs can be acknowledged and met. Here are key aspects to consider when communicating your needs and desires effectively:

Subsection 2.1: Self-Reflection and Clarity

Take time to reflect on your own needs and desires. Be clear about what you want and why it is important to you. Understand your own emotions and motivations behind these needs. This self-reflection helps you communicate your needs more effectively.

Subsection 2.2: Using "I" Statements

Frame your communication using "I" statements to express your needs and desires. Instead of making accusatory or generalizing statements, focus on how you feel and what you personally need. For example, say "I feel..." or "I would like..." This approach takes ownership of your feelings and avoids sounding demanding or critical.

Subsection 2.3: Active Listening and Empathy

Effective communication involves active listening and empathy. Before expressing your needs, ensure that you have actively listened to the other person's perspective and shown empathy. By understanding their viewpoint, you can communicate your needs in a way that respects their feelings and fosters understanding.

Subsection 2.4: Be Specific and Concrete

When expressing your needs and desires, be specific and concrete. Clearly articulate what you are asking for or what you would like to happen. Vague or ambiguous communication can lead to misunderstandings. Providing specific details helps others understand and respond to your needs more effectively.

Subsection 2.5: Consider Timing and Delivery

Choose an appropriate time and place to communicate your needs and desires. Consider the other person's emotional state and readiness to listen. Deliver your message in a calm and respectful manner. Avoid confrontational or demanding tones. Aim for a collaborative and constructive conversation.

Subsection 2.6: Active Problem-Solving

Engage in active problem-solving when discussing your needs. Be open to finding mutually beneficial solutions. Listen to the other person's perspective and collaborate on finding compromises or alternative approaches. Actively seek resolution and work together towards meeting both of your needs.

Subsection 2.7: Respectful Boundaries and Consent

Respect the boundaries and consent of the other person. Understand that they have their own needs and desires as well. Communicate your needs while being mindful of their comfort levels and boundaries. Allow space for negotiation and mutual agreement.

Subsection 2.8: Practice Active Empathy

As you communicate your needs and desires, practice active empathy. Try to understand and appreciate the other person's perspective. Consider their emotions and reactions. By demonstrating empathy, you create an atmosphere of understanding and collaboration.

Section 3: Setting and Respecting Personal Boundaries

Setting and respecting personal boundaries is vital for maintaining healthy relationships and ensuring mutual respect and well-being. Boundaries define acceptable limits, expectations, and behaviors in relationships. Here are key aspects to consider when setting and respecting personal boundaries:

Subsection 3.1: Self-Awareness and Self-Reflection

Develop self-awareness and engage in self-reflection to understand your own needs, limits, and comfort levels. Consider what is important to you, your values, and what you are willing to accept in relationships. This self-awareness forms the foundation for setting and communicating your personal boundaries.

Subsection 3.2: Identify Your Boundaries

Identify and define your boundaries clearly. Recognize what behaviors, actions, or situations make you uncomfortable, violated, or compromised. This could include emotional, physical, or personal space boundaries. Be specific and communicate your boundaries assertively but respectfully.

Subsection 3.3: Communicate Boundaries Clearly

Communicate your boundaries clearly and assertively to others. Use "I" statements to express your limits and expectations. Clearly communicate what you are comfortable with and what you are not. Be direct, honest, and respectful when discussing your boundaries, ensuring open and honest communication.

Subsection 3.4: Listen and Respect Others' Boundaries

While setting your own boundaries, it is equally important to listen and respect others' boundaries. Understand that everyone has their own limits and needs. Actively listen when others communicate their boundaries to you and respect them without judgment or attempts to push past them.

Subsection 3.5: Maintain Consistency

Consistency is key in upholding personal boundaries. Be consistent in your behavior and responses to boundary violations. Communicate and reinforce your boundaries when necessary, and be firm in maintaining them. Consistency helps establish trust and respect within relationships.

Subsection 3.6: Seek Mutual Agreement and Compromise

In certain situations, it may be necessary to negotiate and find compromises regarding boundaries. Engage in open and honest discussions to find a middle ground where both parties' needs are considered and respected. Seek mutual agreement and ensure that boundaries are respected by all involved.

Subsection 3.7: Practice Self-Care

Setting and respecting personal boundaries is a form of self-care. Prioritize your well-being and practice self-care strategies that reinforce your boundaries. Take time for self-reflection, establish healthy habits, and engage in activities that promote your emotional and physical well-being.

Subsection 3.8: Reevaluate and Adjust as Needed

Periodically reevaluate your boundaries and make adjustments as needed. As you grow and change, your boundaries may evolve as well. Regularly assess whether your boundaries are still aligned with your values, needs, and personal growth.

By setting and respecting personal boundaries, you create a foundation of respect, trust, and mutual understanding in your relationships.

Boundaries provide clarity and promote healthy dynamics where both parties feel safe and respected.

Chapter 7: Authenticity in Online Interactions and Social Media

Section 1: The Impact of Digital Communication

Digital communication, including online interactions and social media, has become a significant part of our lives. It offers opportunities for connection and self-expression, but it also poses challenges to maintaining authenticity. Understanding the impact of digital communication is crucial for navigating the digital age while staying true to yourself.

Subsection 1.1: The Influence of Social Media

Recognize the influence of social media on our perceptions and interactions. Social media platforms often emphasize curated versions of ourselves, leading to a potential disconnect between the online persona and our true selves. Be aware of the pressures to present a certain image and seek validation through likes and followers.

Subsection 1.2: Balancing Online and Offline Identity

Find a balance between your online and offline identity. While it's natural to project certain aspects of yourself online, it's important to maintain authenticity by being true to your values and beliefs. Strive for consistency in how you present yourself digitally and offline, ensuring that your online persona reflects who you truly are.

Subsection 1.3: Navigating Digital Relationships

Understand the nuances of digital relationships. Online interactions can be fulfilling, but they can also be prone to miscommunication or misinterpretation. Practice empathy, active listening, and genuine engagement to foster authentic connections in the digital space. Be mindful of the potential for anonymity and the importance of treating others with respect and kindness.

Subsection 1.4: The Perils of Comparison and Self-Worth

Be mindful of the perils of comparison and its impact on self-worth in the digital realm. Social media can create a culture of comparison, leading to feelings of inadequacy or a distorted sense of self. Remember that social media often showcases highlights and curated moments, and it doesn't fully reflect the complexities of real life.

Section 2: Strategies for Maintaining Authenticity Online

Maintaining authenticity in the digital age requires conscious effort and intention. Here are key strategies to consider:

Subsection 2.1: Reflect on Your Intentions

Reflect on your intentions when engaging in digital communication. Ask yourself why you are posting or interacting online. Ensure that your actions align with your values and genuine desire for connection rather than seeking validation or trying to portray a false image.

Subsection 2.2: Be Mindful of Your Digital Footprint

Be mindful of the digital footprint you create. Recognize that your online presence can have long-term consequences. Think before you post or share personal information, images, or opinions. Consider the potential impact on your reputation and personal relationships.

Subsection 2.3: Share Authentically and Responsibly

Share content that is authentic and reflects your true interests, passions, and experiences. Be responsible in what you post and consider the potential impact on others. Avoid engaging in online behaviors that promote dishonesty, cyberbullying, or negativity.

Subsection 2.4: Cultivate Meaningful Connections

Focus on cultivating meaningful connections rather than chasing popularity or numbers. Engage with others genuinely and seek to build authentic relationships online. Quality interactions with a few like-minded individuals can be more fulfilling than shallow connections with a large number of followers.

Subsection 2.5: Practice Digital Detox

Take regular breaks from digital platforms to recharge and reconnect with the offline world. Disconnecting from social media and online interactions can help you recenter yourself, reduce comparison, and refocus on your own values and goals.

Subsection 2.6: Embrace Vulnerability and Imperfection

Embrace vulnerability and allow yourself to be imperfect online. Share your challenges, failures, and lessons learned along with your achievements. Embracing vulnerability fosters authenticity and encourages others to do the same.

Subsection 2.7: Authentic Engagement and Empathy

Engage authentically with others by being present, attentive, and empathetic. Practice active listening and respond thoughtfully. Show genuine interest in others' perspectives, experiences, and emotions. Be supportive, respectful, and kind in your digital interactions.

Section 3: Honoring Your Authenticity in the Digital Age

In the digital age, it's crucial to honor your authenticity as you navigate the online landscape. Staying true to yourself in the midst of digital communication can be challenging, but with the right techniques and approaches, you can maintain your authenticity. Here are practical steps for honoring your authenticity in the digital age:

Subsection 3.1: Self-Reflection and Values Alignment

Engage in self-reflection to gain a deeper understanding of your values, beliefs, and personal boundaries. Take time to identify what matters most to you and how you want to show up in the digital space. Align your online presence with your authentic self by making intentional choices that reflect your values.

Subsection 3.2: Curating Your Digital Persona

While it's important to be authentic, curating your digital persona can help align your online presence with your values and goals. Choose the content you share carefully, ensuring that it reflects your true interests and passions. Be mindful of the impact your online persona has on others and strive for authenticity in your interactions.

Subsection 3.3: Mindful Social Media Use

Practice mindful social media use by being intentional about the platforms you engage with and the content you consume. Regularly evaluate the impact of social media on your well-being and make adjustments as necessary. Create boundaries around your social media usage to maintain a healthy balance between the online world and real-life experiences.

Subsection 3.4: Authentic Engagement

Engage authentically with others by fostering genuine connections and meaningful conversations. Respond thoughtfully, showing interest and empathy. Avoid engaging in performative behavior or seeking validation through likes and comments. Focus on building relationships based on shared values and mutual respect.

Subsection 3.5: Digital Detox and Self-Care

Take regular digital detoxes to recharge and prioritize self-care. Disconnecting from the online world allows you to reconnect with yourself, your emotions, and your offline relationships. Use this time to engage in activities that bring you joy, nurture your well-being, and foster authentic connections in the real world.

Subsection 3.6: Honoring Privacy and Security

Respect your privacy and security online by being mindful of the information you share. Set appropriate privacy settings on your social media accounts and be cautious about the personal details you disclose. Protect your online identity and be aware of potential risks associated with sharing sensitive information.

Subsection 3.7: Authentic Contribution

Contribute to online communities and conversations authentically. Share your knowledge, experiences, and perspectives in a genuine and respectful manner. Offer constructive feedback and support to others. By adding value to digital spaces through your authentic contributions, you can foster meaningful connections and establish yourself as a trusted presence.

Subsection 3.8: Continual Self-Reflection and Growth

Engage in continual self-reflection and growth as you navigate the digital landscape. Regularly reassess your online presence, interactions, and the impact they have on yourself and others. Adapt and refine your approach as you learn and grow. Stay open to feedback and strive to continually align your online presence with your evolving authentic self.

By implementing these practical steps, you can honor your authenticity in the digital age. Remember that authenticity is a lifelong journey, and it requires consistent self-awareness and intentional choices. Embrace your unique voice, values, and experiences as you engage in digital communication, and you will foster genuine connections and relationships online.

Section 4: Building Genuine Connections Online

Building genuine connections online is a valuable skill in the digital age. While the online world can sometimes feel disconnected, it is possible to cultivate meaningful relationships through authentic interactions. Here are key aspects to consider when building genuine connections online:

Subsection 4.1: Authentic Self-Presentation

Present yourself authentically online by being true to who you are. Avoid creating a façade or pretending to be someone you're not. Be honest about your interests, values, and experiences. By presenting yourself authentically, you attract like-minded individuals who resonate with your true self.

Subsection 4.2: Engaging in Genuine Dialogue

Engage in genuine dialogue with others by actively listening and responding thoughtfully. Avoid superficial or generic responses. Show genuine interest in the opinions, thoughts, and experiences of others. Ask open-ended questions and encourage deeper conversations.

Subsection 4.3: Sharing Personal Stories and Experiences

Share personal stories and experiences that reflect your authentic self. Vulnerability can be a catalyst for genuine connections. By opening up and sharing your journey, you invite others to do the same and create a space for meaningful connections to flourish.

Subsection 4.4: Supporting and Encouraging Others

Be supportive and encouraging to others in the online community. Offer words of kindness, empathy, and validation. Celebrate their successes and provide support during challenging times. Authentic connections are built on a foundation of mutual support and encouragement.

Subsection 4.5: Finding Common Interests and Values

Seek out communities and platforms where you can connect with individuals who share common interests and values. Engage in discussions, forums, or groups centered around topics that resonate with you. These shared interests and values form a strong basis for building genuine connections.

Subsection 4.6: Practicing Digital Empathy

Practice digital empathy by considering the perspectives and emotions of others. Be mindful of the impact your words and actions can have on someone's well-being. Show kindness, respect, and understanding in your interactions. By practicing empathy, you create a safe and supportive environment for genuine connections.

Subsection 4.7: Investing Time and Effort

Building genuine connections online requires time and effort. Dedicate quality time to engage with others, respond to messages, and participate in conversations. Genuine connections are nurtured through consistent and meaningful interactions.

Subsection 4.8: Transitioning to Offline Interactions

When appropriate and comfortable, consider transitioning online connections to offline interactions. Meet up in person or engage in video calls to deepen the connection beyond the digital realm. Face-to-face interactions can strengthen the authenticity and depth of the relationship.

Section 5: Navigating Social Media While Staying True to Yourself

Navigating social media while staying true to yourself requires mindful awareness and intentional choices. It's important to engage with social media platforms in a way that aligns with your values and authentic self-expression. Here are practical strategies for navigating social media while staying true to yourself:

Subsection 5.1: Define Your Social Media Purpose

Clarify your purpose for using social media. Identify what you hope to achieve, whether it's connecting with like-minded individuals, sharing your passions, or staying informed. By defining your purpose, you can ensure that your social media usage serves your authentic goals and values.

Subsection 5.2: Curate Your Social Media Feed

Curate your social media feed to align with your interests and values. Follow accounts and communities that inspire and uplift you, and unfollow or mute those that contribute to negativity or undermine your authenticity. Surround yourself with content that reflects your authentic self and encourages personal growth.

Subsection 5.3: Practice Mindful Consumption

Be mindful of the content you consume on social media. Take regular breaks to assess how the content impacts your emotions and overall well-being. Avoid mindlessly scrolling and engage with intention. Consciously choose to interact with posts and discussions that resonate with your authentic self.

Subsection 5.4: Share Meaningful Content

Share content on social media that reflects your passions, interests, and values. Be genuine and purposeful in your posts, captions, and comments. Avoid seeking validation or approval through likes and followers. Focus on sharing what truly matters to you and contributing meaningfully to the online community.

Subsection 5.5: Cultivate Authentic Connections

Prioritize cultivating authentic connections on social media. Engage in genuine conversations, offer support, and celebrate others' achievements. Take the time to build relationships based on trust, respect, and shared interests. Authentic connections are more valuable than a large following, and they contribute to a more fulfilling online experience.

Subsection 5.6: Embrace Vulnerability

Embrace vulnerability on social media by sharing your authentic experiences, challenges, and growth. Show the human side of yourself and open up about your journey. This allows others to connect with you on a deeper level and creates a space for genuine conversations and support.

Subsection 5.7: Set Digital Boundaries

Establish boundaries for your social media usage. Determine how much time you want to spend on social media and when it's appropriate to disconnect. Be mindful of the impact social media has on your mental health and well-being. Set boundaries to protect your authenticity and prioritize self-care.

Subsection 5.8: Regular Self-Reflection

Engage in regular self-reflection to assess your relationship with social media. Reflect on how it aligns with your values and whether it enhances or detracts from your authentic self-expression. Adjust your social media habits and practices as needed to maintain authenticity and ensure a healthy digital experience.

By navigating social media with mindfulness, intentionality, and self-awareness, you can stay true to yourself while engaging in the digital world. Remember to prioritize meaningful connections, practice authenticity, and set boundaries that support your well-being.

Chapter 8: Cultivating Shared Interests and Experiences

Section 1: The Importance of Shared Interests in Relationships

Shared interests and passions play a significant role in building connections and fostering meaningful relationships. When you find common ground with someone, it creates a sense of connection, understanding, and shared experiences. Here are key aspects to consider regarding the importance of shared interests in relationships:

Subsection 1.1: Building a Foundation

Shared interests provide a foundation for connection and conversation. When you have common ground with someone, it becomes easier to engage in discussions, share experiences, and explore mutual passions. It acts as a starting point for building rapport and deepening your connection.

Subsection 1.2: Enhancing Communication

Shared interests enhance communication by providing topics that both parties are enthusiastic about. It creates an opportunity for meaningful conversations and the exchange of ideas. When you share a passion, it becomes a natural bridge to connect and engage with each other on a deeper level.

Subsection 1.3: Creating Lasting Memories

Engaging in shared interests and experiences allows you to create lasting memories together. Whether it's exploring a shared hobby, attending events, or embarking on adventures, these shared experiences create a bond and contribute to the strength of your relationship.

Subsection 1.4: Fostering Connection and Understanding

Shared interests foster connection and understanding between individuals. When you both share a passion, it provides insight into each other's values, preferences, and perspectives. It allows for a deeper understanding of each other's identities and contributes to a sense of camaraderie.

Subsection 1.5: Supporting Each Other's Growth

Shared interests offer an opportunity to support each other's personal growth. By engaging in activities that you both enjoy, you can provide encouragement, motivation, and feedback. Supporting each other's pursuits strengthens the relationship and helps both individuals thrive.

Section 2: Finding Common Ground and Shared Passions

Finding common ground and shared passions requires exploration and open-mindedness. Here are practical strategies to consider when seeking shared interests with someone:

Subsection 2.1: Engage in Active Listening

Listen actively to the other person's interests and passions. Pay attention to what excites them and what activities they enjoy. By actively listening, you gain insights into their preferences and can identify potential areas of shared interest.

Subsection 2.2: Share Your Own Passions

Share your own passions and interests openly. By expressing what brings you joy and enthusiasm, you provide an opportunity for the other person to connect with you on a deeper level. Your genuine enthusiasm can spark curiosity and potential shared interests.

Subsection 2.3: Explore New Activities Together

Be open to exploring new activities together. Engage in experiences that neither of you has tried before. This opens up opportunities to discover shared passions and allows for a sense of adventure and growth in the relationship.

Subsection 2.4: Attend Events and Workshops

Attend events, workshops, or classes related to your interests. These provide an environment where you can meet others who share similar passions. By participating in these activities together, you increase the chances of finding shared interests and connecting with like-minded individuals.

Subsection 2.5: Volunteer or Join Communities

Volunteer or join communities centered around a cause or interest that aligns with your values. This allows you to meet individuals who share your passions and provides a platform for engaging in meaningful activities together.

Subsection 2.6: Encourage Open Exploration

Encourage each other to explore new interests and hobbies. Support each other's curiosity and encourage a spirit of adventure. By embracing new experiences together, you create opportunities to find shared passions and deepen your connection.

Subsection 2.7: Embrace Differences

Acknowledge and appreciate that you may have different interests and passions. Embracing each other's individuality enriches the relationship and allows for a healthy balance of shared and independent pursuits. Respect and support each other's unique passions, even if they differ from your own.

Subsection 2.8: Prioritize Quality Time

Allocate dedicated quality time to engage in activities related to your shared interests. Make it a priority to nurture your connection by regularly participating in shared experiences. This strengthens the bond and creates opportunities for deeper conversations and shared memories.

By actively seeking and cultivating shared interests and experiences, you can deepen your connection with someone and enhance the quality of your relationship. Remember to approach this process with an open mind, embrace each other's individuality, and enjoy the journey of exploration and discovery together.

Section 3: Participating in Activities Together

Participating in activities together strengthens the bond between individuals and creates shared experiences that contribute to the growth of the relationship. Engaging in joint activities allows for shared enjoyment, learning, and the creation of lasting memories. Here are practical strategies for participating in activities together:

Subsection 3.1: Explore Each Other's Interests

Take turns exploring each other's interests and passions. Encourage each other to share activities that they enjoy and would like to experience together. This allows for a broader range of shared activities and provides an opportunity to learn more about each other's hobbies and preferences.

Subsection 3.2: Plan and Prioritize Quality Time

Allocate dedicated time for participating in activities together. Make it a priority to set aside regular quality time to engage in shared interests. This demonstrates your commitment to the relationship and creates opportunities for bonding and connection.

Subsection 3.3: Try New Activities

Be open to trying new activities that neither of you has experienced before. Embrace the opportunity for exploration and adventure. Trying new things together fosters a sense of excitement and allows you to discover shared interests that may have been previously unknown.

Subsection 3.4: Create Rituals and Traditions

Establish rituals and traditions around shared activities. These can be weekly date nights, monthly outings, or annual events that hold significance for both of you. Creating these shared rituals strengthens the bond and provides a sense of continuity and anticipation in the relationship.

Subsection 3.5: Engage in Active and Outdoor Pursuits

Participate in active and outdoor pursuits together. This could include hiking, biking, playing sports, or engaging in physical fitness activities. Active pursuits not only promote health and well-being but also provide an opportunity for shared adventure and mutual support.

Subsection 3.6: Attend Cultural and Artistic Events

Explore cultural and artistic events in your community, such as concerts, exhibitions, theater performances, or film screenings. Attend these events together to appreciate and discuss the shared experience. Engaging in cultural activities broadens your horizons and deepens your connection.

Subsection 3.7: Take Classes or Learn a New Skill

Enroll in classes or workshops that align with your mutual interests or a skill you both want to learn. This could be cooking, dancing, painting, or any other shared interest. Learning together fosters growth, encourages teamwork, and creates opportunities for shared achievement.

Subsection 3.8: Volunteer and Give Back

Engage in volunteer activities or community service together. Contributing to a cause that both of you care about strengthens your bond and allows you to make a positive impact as a team. Volunteering fosters shared values and a sense of purpose in the relationship.

By actively participating in activities together, you create shared experiences that contribute to the growth and strength of your relationship. These shared moments foster connection, deepen understanding, and create lasting memories. Prioritize quality time, explore new interests, and embrace the adventure of experiencing life together.

Section 4: Creating Memories and Meaningful Experiences

Creating memories and meaningful experiences is an essential aspect of building lasting relationships. These shared moments contribute to the depth and emotional connection between individuals. Here are practical strategies for creating memories and meaningful experiences together:

Subsection 4.1: Be Present in the Moment

Practice being fully present in the activities and experiences you share. Put away distractions, such as smartphones or work-related thoughts, and focus on engaging with each other and the experience at hand. By immersing yourself in the present moment, you create space for genuine connection and the formation of meaningful memories.

Subsection 4.2: Embrace Spontaneity and Adventure

Embrace spontaneity and inject adventure into your shared experiences. Step out of your comfort zone and try new things together. Take spontaneous trips, explore unfamiliar places, or engage in activities that challenge and excite both of you. These adventures create memorable moments and strengthen your bond.

Subsection 4.3: Capture and Document Moments

Capture and document your shared moments through photographs, videos, or journaling. These tangible reminders allow you to revisit and relive the experiences, evoking the emotions and memories associated with them. Reflecting on these captured moments can deepen your connection and serve as a source of joy and nostalgia.

Subsection 4.4: Celebrate Milestones and Special Occasions

Celebrate milestones, anniversaries, and special occasions together. Create rituals and traditions around these events to make them even more meaningful. These celebratory moments provide opportunities to express love, appreciation, and gratitude for each other, fostering a sense of connection and shared joy.

Subsection 4.5: Engage in Meaningful Conversations

Engage in deep, meaningful conversations during your shared experiences. Discuss your hopes, dreams, fears, and aspirations. Share your thoughts, values, and beliefs. By having open and honest conversations, you create opportunities for emotional intimacy and a deeper understanding of each other.

Subsection 4.6: Nurture Shared Hobbies and Interests

Nurture shared hobbies and interests over time. Continuously invest in activities that bring you both joy and fulfillment. Engaging in these shared passions allows you to bond over common experiences and grow together in areas that you are both passionate about.

Subsection 4.7: Create Personal Traditions

Establish personal traditions that are unique to your relationship. These could be regular date nights, annual trips, or monthly activities that hold special meaning for both of you. Personal traditions provide a sense of continuity and create a shared narrative that strengthens your connection.

Subsection 4.8: Practice Gratitude

Express gratitude for the experiences and memories you create together. Acknowledge and appreciate the joy and growth that come from shared moments. Gratitude enhances the emotional connection and fosters a positive perspective on your shared experiences.

By actively creating memories and meaningful experiences, you infuse your relationship with moments of joy, growth, and connection. Embrace the present moment, celebrate milestones, engage in deep conversations, and nurture shared interests. These intentional efforts will help build a foundation of cherished memories that deepen your bond and create a fulfilling relationship.

Chapter 9: Nurturing Emotional Intimacy and Connection

Section 1: The Importance of Emotional Intimacy in Relationships

Emotional intimacy forms the foundation of deep and meaningful connections. It involves mutual understanding, vulnerability, and trust, and it allows individuals to truly know and be known by their partners. Here are key aspects to consider regarding the importance of emotional intimacy in relationships:

Subsection 1.1: Building Trust and Safety

Emotional intimacy requires trust and safety within the relationship. Create an environment where both partners feel secure to express their thoughts, feelings, and fears without judgment or rejection. Building trust fosters a deeper emotional connection and allows for the vulnerability needed to nurture emotional intimacy.

Subsection 1.2: Enhancing Communication

Effective communication is essential for nurturing emotional intimacy. Practice active listening, empathy, and non-judgmental responses to create a space where both partners can freely express themselves. Encourage open and honest communication, and be attentive to each other's emotional needs and cues.

Subsection 1.3: Cultivating Empathy and Understanding

Develop empathy and understanding for each other's experiences, emotions, and perspectives. Seek to truly comprehend your partner's point of view and validate their feelings. By demonstrating empathy, you foster a deeper emotional connection and create a supportive and compassionate bond.

Subsection 1.4: Encouraging Emotional Expression

Encourage emotional expression and authenticity within the relationship. Create an environment where both partners feel comfortable sharing their true thoughts and emotions. Validate and support each other's emotional experiences, allowing for a deeper connection and emotional intimacy to flourish.

Section 2: Deepening Emotional Connection Over Time

Building and deepening emotional connection is an ongoing process that requires intentional effort and nurturing. Here are practical strategies for deepening emotional connection over time:

Subsection 2.1: Engage in Meaningful Conversations

Engage in regular, meaningful conversations that explore each other's hopes, dreams, and fears. Make time to discuss deeper aspects of your lives and share your innermost thoughts and emotions. These conversations cultivate emotional intimacy and allow for a deeper understanding of each other.

Subsection 2.2: Practice Active Listening and Validation

Practice active listening by giving your partner your full attention and being present in the moment. Validate their feelings and experiences, showing that you understand and empathize. By actively listening and validating, you demonstrate your commitment to deepening emotional connection and fostering intimacy.

Subsection 2.3: Share Vulnerabilities and Past Experiences

Share vulnerabilities and past experiences with each other. Opening up about personal challenges, fears, and past hurts creates a space for emotional connection and understanding. By being vulnerable, you invite your partner to reciprocate and deepen the emotional bond between you.

Subsection 2.4: Create Rituals of Connection

Establish rituals that facilitate emotional connection and intimacy. This could include regular date nights, shared activities, or meaningful gestures that demonstrate love and appreciation. Consistently engaging in these rituals strengthens the emotional connection and serves as a reminder of your commitment to each other.

Subsection 2.5: Support Each Other's Emotional Well-Being

Prioritize each other's emotional well-being by offering support, comfort, and encouragement. Be attentive to your partner's emotional needs and provide a safe space for them to express their emotions. Supporting each other emotionally strengthens the bond and builds trust within the relationship.

Subsection 2.6: Engage in Shared Activities and Experiences

Continue to engage in shared activities and experiences that foster emotional connection. Create new memories together and revisit past ones. These shared experiences deepen the emotional bond and create a shared narrative that strengthens your connection over time.

Subsection 2.7: Seek Couples Therapy or Counseling

If needed, consider seeking couples therapy or counseling to enhance your emotional connection. A professional can guide you in exploring and resolving underlying issues that may hinder emotional intimacy. Couples therapy provides a safe and supportive environment to nurture your emotional connection.

Subsection 2.8: Embrace Growth and Change Together

Embrace personal growth and change as individuals and as a couple. Support each other's personal development and encourage self-reflection. By growing together and embracing change, you create opportunities for deeper emotional connection and an evolving and fulfilling relationship.

By actively nurturing emotional intimacy and deepening the emotional connection over time, you create a strong foundation for a fulfilling and lasting relationship. Prioritize trust, effective communication, empathy, and vulnerability. Engage in meaningful conversations, share vulnerabilities, and support each other's emotional well-being. These efforts contribute to a deep and meaningful emotional connection with your partner.

Section 3: Sharing Vulnerable Moments and Experiences

Sharing vulnerable moments and experiences is a powerful way to deepen emotional intimacy and strengthen the connection between partners. It requires trust, empathy, and a willingness to be open and authentic. Here are practical strategies for sharing vulnerable moments and experiences:

Subsection 3.1: Cultivating Trust and Safety

Build a foundation of trust and safety within the relationship. Create an environment where both partners feel comfortable expressing vulnerability without fear of judgment or rejection. Trust provides a solid framework for sharing vulnerable moments and experiences.

Subsection 3.2: Practice Active Listening and Empathy

Engage in active listening when your partner shares vulnerable moments or experiences. Give them your full attention, show empathy, and validate their feelings. Let them know that you are present and supportive during these vulnerable moments.

Subsection 3.3: Share Your Own Vulnerabilities

Lead by example and share your own vulnerabilities with your partner. By opening up and expressing your own challenges and insecurities, you create a safe space for your partner to do the same. This reciprocity fosters trust and deepens the emotional connection between both of you.

Subsection 3.4: Encourage Non-Judgmental Communication

Create an atmosphere of non-judgmental communication where both partners feel free to express themselves authentically. Avoid criticizing or dismissing each other's vulnerabilities and experiences. Instead, offer understanding, compassion, and support.

Subsection 3.5: Reflect on Past Growth and Lessons

Reflect on past growth and lessons learned from vulnerable moments or challenging experiences. Share how these experiences have shaped you and contributed to your personal growth. This reflection deepens the emotional connection and allows for shared understanding and growth as a couple.

Subsection 3.6: Seek Emotional Support from Each Other

Offer emotional support to your partner when they share vulnerable moments or experiences. Listen actively, provide comfort, and offer reassurance. Create a space where they feel understood and validated, and reciprocate by being there for them during your own vulnerable moments.

Subsection 3.7: Practice Forgiveness and Acceptance

Practice forgiveness and acceptance when sharing vulnerable moments and experiences. Understand that vulnerability can sometimes lead to mistakes or missteps. Show compassion, let go of resentment, and work towards understanding and growth together.

Subsection 3.8: Seek Professional Help if Needed

If necessary, consider seeking the support of a couples therapist or counselor. A trained professional can guide you in navigating vulnerable moments and experiences, providing tools and strategies to deepen emotional intimacy and strengthen your connection.

By sharing vulnerable moments and experiences, you create a deeper level of emotional intimacy and understanding in your relationship. Prioritize trust, active listening, empathy, and non-judgmental communication. Share your vulnerabilities, offer support, and embrace the growth that comes from these shared experiences. These efforts foster a stronger emotional bond and cultivate a lasting and fulfilling relationship.

Section 4: Strengthening the Emotional Bond

Strengthening the emotional bond between partners is crucial for building a resilient and fulfilling relationship. It involves fostering a deep sense of connection, trust, and understanding. Here are practical strategies for strengthening the emotional bond:

Subsection 4.1: Prioritize Quality Time

Allocate dedicated quality time for each other regularly. Make it a priority to engage in activities that foster emotional connection and intimacy. This dedicated time allows you to nurture your bond and deepen your understanding of each other.

Subsection 4.2: Practice Active and Attentive Listening

Engage in active and attentive listening when your partner speaks. Focus on their words, tone, and non-verbal cues. Demonstrate genuine interest in what they have to say, allowing them to feel heard and understood. Active listening strengthens the emotional bond and enhances communication.

Subsection 4.3: Express Love and Appreciation

Regularly express love and appreciation to your partner. Verbalize your affection, acknowledge their efforts, and express gratitude for their presence in your life. These acts of love and appreciation reinforce the emotional bond and create a positive and nurturing atmosphere.

Subsection 4.4: Practice Empathy and Understanding

Cultivate empathy and understanding in your relationship. Put yourself in your partner's shoes and strive to comprehend their emotions, perspectives, and experiences. Show empathy by validating their feelings and providing support during challenging times. This deepens the emotional connection and fosters a sense of togetherness.

Subsection 4.5: Share Personal Dreams and Goals

Share your personal dreams, goals, and aspirations with each other. Openly discuss your visions for the future and the role you envision each other playing in achieving those goals. Sharing personal dreams fosters a sense of partnership and strengthens the emotional bond by aligning your aspirations.

Subsection 4.6: Foster Emotional Intimacy through Physical Touch

Physical touch plays a significant role in nurturing emotional intimacy. Engage in affectionate gestures, such as hugging, cuddling, holding hands, or gentle touches. Physical touch releases oxytocin, the bonding hormone, and deepens the emotional connection between partners.

Subsection 4.7: Support Each Other's Emotional Well-Being

Provide support and encouragement for each other's emotional well-being. Be attentive to your partner's needs, offer a listening ear, and provide comfort during challenging times. Supporting each other emotionally strengthens the bond and creates a sense of safety and security.

Subsection 4.8: Engage in Shared Reflection and Growth

Engage in shared reflection and growth as individuals and as a couple. Regularly assess your relationship dynamics, identify areas for improvement, and commit to personal and joint growth. By continuously investing in personal development and relationship enhancement, you strengthen the emotional bond over time.

Subsection 4.9: Seek Relationship Enrichment Resources

Explore relationship enrichment resources such as books, workshops, or couples therapy. These resources provide guidance, tools, and techniques to deepen emotional connection and strengthen the bond. Seeking outside support demonstrates your commitment to the relationship and growth as a couple.

By actively implementing these strategies, you can strengthen the emotional bond and foster a deeper connection with your partner. Prioritize quality time, practice active listening, express love and appreciation, and foster empathy and understanding. Engage in shared reflection, support each other's emotional well-being, and seek resources that enhance your relationship. These efforts contribute to a resilient and fulfilling emotional bond.

Chapter 10: Sustaining Authentic Relationships: Challenges and Growth

Section 1: The Nature of Challenges and Conflicts in Relationships

Challenges and conflicts are a natural part of any relationship. They can arise from differences in perspectives, needs, and expectations. However, navigating these challenges authentically can lead to growth and deeper connection. Here are key aspects to consider regarding challenges and conflicts in relationships:

Subsection 1.1: Understanding the Purpose of Challenges

Challenges in relationships provide opportunities for growth, learning, and understanding. They can strengthen the bond between partners when approached with authenticity and a commitment to resolving conflicts in a healthy and constructive manner.

Subsection 1.2: Embracing Open Communication

Open communication is vital when facing challenges and conflicts. It involves expressing thoughts, feelings, and concerns honestly and respectfully. By fostering an environment of open communication, you create space for understanding, compromise, and resolution.

Subsection 1.3: Accepting Individual Differences

Accepting and embracing individual differences is crucial in overcoming challenges and conflicts. Each partner brings their unique experiences, perspectives, and values to the relationship. By acknowledging and respecting these differences, you can navigate conflicts with empathy and understanding.

Subsection 1.4: Seeking Common Ground

Finding common ground is essential when addressing challenges and conflicts. Identifying shared goals, values, or interests can help bridge gaps and facilitate effective problem-solving. By focusing on shared objectives, you can work together to overcome obstacles and strengthen the relationship.

Section 2: Overcoming Challenges and Conflicts Authentically

Authenticity plays a significant role in resolving challenges and conflicts in relationships. It involves staying true to yourself, expressing your needs and boundaries, and actively engaging in the resolution process. Here are practical strategies for overcoming challenges and conflicts authentically:

Subsection 2.1: Practice Active Listening and Empathy

Listen actively to your partner's perspective during conflicts. Demonstrate empathy by seeking to understand their point of view. By actively listening and showing empathy, you create a safe space for open dialogue and foster a deeper connection.

Subsection 2.2: Express Feelings and Needs Authentically

Be honest and authentic when expressing your feelings and needs during conflicts. Use "I" statements to communicate how specific situations or behaviors impact you. Avoid blaming or criticizing your partner and focus on expressing your emotions and desires constructively.

Subsection 2.3: Embrace Vulnerability

Embrace vulnerability by sharing your fears, insecurities, and concerns during conflicts. Opening up authentically allows your partner to understand your perspective and fosters a sense of trust and connection. Vulnerability can lead to deeper understanding and resolution.

Subsection 2.4: Seek Win-Win Solutions

Strive for win-win solutions that honor the needs and perspectives of both partners. Collaborate in finding creative solutions that address the underlying issues and support the growth of the relationship. By seeking mutually beneficial outcomes, you create a foundation for sustainable resolution.

Subsection 2.5: Practice Forgiveness and Letting Go

Forgiveness and letting go are essential in resolving conflicts authentically. Holding onto grudges or past hurts can hinder the growth and healing of the relationship. Practice forgiveness, both for yourself and your partner, and work towards moving forward with a clean slate.

Subsection 2.6: Seek Mediation or Couples Therapy

If conflicts persist or become overwhelming, consider seeking the support of a mediator or couples therapist. A trained professional can facilitate healthy communication, provide guidance, and offer tools for conflict resolution. Seeking outside help shows a commitment to growth and the well-being of the relationship.

Subsection 2.7: Learn and Grow from Challenges

View challenges and conflicts as opportunities for personal and relationship growth. Reflect on the lessons learned and seek to apply them in future situations. Approach challenges with a growth mindset, knowing that overcoming them authentically can strengthen the bond between partners.

Subsection 2.8: Cultivate a Culture of Appreciation

Foster a culture of appreciation within the relationship, even during challenging times. Express gratitude for your partner's efforts, strengths, and qualities. Recognize and acknowledge the progress made in resolving conflicts authentically. Cultivating appreciation contributes to a positive and resilient relationship.

By approaching challenges and conflicts authentically, you can navigate them with empathy, understanding, and growth in mind. Practice open communication, embrace vulnerability, and seek win-win solutions. Foster forgiveness, seek outside help if needed, and cultivate a culture of appreciation. These efforts contribute to sustaining an authentic and thriving relationship.

Section 3: Continuously Growing Together

Continuously growing together as individuals and as a couple is essential for maintaining a thriving and authentic relationship. It involves a commitment to personal development, shared goals, and ongoing communication. Here are practical strategies for continuous growth:

Subsection 3.1: Embrace Personal Development

Embrace personal development as individuals within the relationship. Foster a growth mindset and engage in activities that promote self-improvement and self-awareness. This includes pursuing hobbies, learning new skills, seeking personal fulfillment, and setting goals for personal growth.

Subsection 3.2: Communicate about Individual Goals and Aspirations

Engage in open and honest communication about your individual goals, aspirations, and dreams. Share your visions for personal growth and discuss how these aspirations align with the shared goals of the relationship. By understanding each other's desires, you can support each other's growth and cultivate a sense of shared purpose.

Subsection 3.3: Prioritize Shared Experiences and Learning

Prioritize shared experiences and learning opportunities as a couple. Engage in activities that foster growth, such as attending workshops, exploring new places, or pursuing joint hobbies. Actively seek opportunities to learn and grow together, creating shared memories and deepening your connection.

Subsection 3.4: Practice Active Reflection and Evaluation

Regularly reflect on your individual and shared experiences. Evaluate what is working well and identify areas for improvement. Discuss your observations openly and collaboratively. This process allows you to adapt, make necessary adjustments, and continue growing together.

Subsection 3.5: Support Each Other's Growth

Support each other's growth by providing encouragement, understanding, and resources. Celebrate each other's achievements and milestones. Create an environment that fosters personal development and empowers each other to reach their full potential.

Subsection 3.6: Seek New Challenges and Adventures

Embrace new challenges and adventures together. Step out of your comfort zones and explore unfamiliar territory. This can involve travel, trying new activities, or taking on joint projects. By venturing into the unknown, you encourage personal growth and strengthen the bond between you.

Subsection 3.7: Engage in Ongoing Communication

Maintain ongoing communication about your personal growth journeys. Share your progress, insights, and challenges. Stay attuned to each other's needs, dreams, and aspirations. Regularly check in on how you can support each other's growth and ensure that you are growing together as a couple.

Subsection 3.8: Seek Professional Support if Needed

If you encounter significant challenges or feel stuck in your personal growth or as a couple, consider seeking the assistance of a relationship coach or therapist. A professional can provide guidance, tools, and support to navigate obstacles and foster continuous growth.

Subsection 3.9: Embrace Adaptability and Flexibility

Embrace adaptability and flexibility as you grow individually and as a couple. Recognize that personal growth journeys are not linear, and priorities may shift over time. Allow room for adjustments, evolving aspirations, and new opportunities as you continue to grow together.

By prioritizing personal development, open communication, and shared experiences, you can foster continuous growth as individuals and as a couple. Embrace personal development, communicate about goals, support each other's growth, seek new challenges, and remain adaptable. Through ongoing growth, you cultivate a vibrant and evolving relationship that thrives on mutual growth and shared experiences.

Section 4: The Lifelong Journey of Building and Sustaining Authentic Relationships

Building and sustaining authentic relationships is a lifelong journey that requires dedication, effort, and continuous learning. It involves embracing the ebb and flow of relationships, adapting to changing circumstances, and nurturing the connection between partners. Here are key aspects to consider regarding the lifelong journey of building and sustaining authentic relationships:

Subsection 4.1: Embrace the Evolution of Relationships

Acknowledge that relationships evolve and change over time. Embrace the different stages, transitions, and challenges that arise. Understand that growth and transformation are natural and that embracing these changes is essential for building a lasting and authentic relationship.

Subsection 4.2: Prioritize Relationship Maintenance

Maintain an active focus on the relationship by prioritizing its care and nurturing. Regularly engage in open and honest communication, quality time together, and acts of love and appreciation. Continuously invest in the relationship to sustain its authenticity and vitality.

Subsection 4.3: Foster Emotional Intimacy

Continue to foster emotional intimacy throughout the relationship. Deepen your understanding of each other's needs, desires, and vulnerabilities. Practice empathy, active listening, and support to create a safe and loving space for emotional connection to flourish.

Subsection 4.4: Cultivate Trust and Honesty

Nurture trust and honesty as foundational elements of the relationship. Be transparent, reliable, and trustworthy in your words and actions. Foster an environment where both partners feel secure and can be authentic with each other.

Subsection 4.5: Embrace Compromise and Collaboration

Recognize that compromise and collaboration are essential for sustaining an authentic relationship. Practice active problem-solving, seek win-win solutions, and make joint decisions that honor the needs and aspirations of both partners. Embrace the value of teamwork and shared responsibility.

Subsection 4.6: Practice Forgiveness and Letting Go

Practice forgiveness and let go of past resentments and grievances. Holding onto grudges can hinder the growth and authenticity of the relationship. Cultivate forgiveness, compassion, and the ability to move forward with love and understanding.

Subsection 4.7: Continuously Learn and Grow

Commit to lifelong learning and personal growth, both individually and as a couple. Seek opportunities for self-reflection, self-improvement, and relationship enrichment. Engage in activities that foster personal and collective growth, allowing the relationship to thrive and evolve.

Subsection 4.8: Embrace Openness and Vulnerability

Continue to embrace openness and vulnerability as the relationship progresses. Share your thoughts, feelings, and fears with your partner. Allow yourselves to be seen and known fully. By maintaining vulnerability, you deepen the authenticity and connection in your relationship.

Subsection 4.9: Seek Support and Seek Help

Acknowledge that seeking support and professional help is a sign of strength and commitment. If challenges arise that feel overwhelming or if you desire additional guidance, consider seeking the assistance of a therapist or relationship coach. They can provide valuable tools, insights, and support along your journey.

The journey of building and sustaining authentic relationships is a lifelong endeavor. Embrace the evolution of relationships, prioritize relationship maintenance, and foster emotional intimacy. Cultivate trust, embrace compromise, and practice forgiveness. Continuously learn and grow, embrace openness and vulnerability, and seek support when needed. By embracing this lifelong journey, you create the opportunity for a fulfilling, authentic, and lasting relationship.

Conclusion:

Building and sustaining authentic relationships with women is a rewarding and lifelong journey. It requires dedication, effort, and a commitment to continuous growth and learning. Throughout this book, we have explored the importance of authenticity in forming meaningful connections, the significance of active listening, vulnerability, and empathy in building trust and creating a safe space for open communication. We have delved into the power of shared experiences, emotional intimacy, and the role of authenticity in overcoming challenges and conflicts.

By prioritizing open and honest communication, practicing empathy and active listening, and nurturing emotional intimacy, you can cultivate a deep and authentic connection with the women in your life. Additionally, embracing personal growth, fostering a culture of support and understanding, and seeking professional help when needed, you can sustain and nourish these relationships over time.

Remember that building and sustaining authentic relationships is a journey that requires ongoing effort and adaptability. Embrace the ebb and flow of relationships, be open to growth and change, and continuously work towards deepening your connection and understanding. Through authenticity, empathy, and a commitment to mutual growth, you can create meaningful and lasting relationships that bring joy, fulfillment, and love.

May this book serve as a guide to inspire and empower you on your journey of building authentic connections and nurturing lasting relationships with women. Embrace the lessons learned and apply them in your interactions, knowing that the rewards of genuine and authentic connections are immeasurable.

Don't miss out!

Visit the website below and you can sign up to receive emails whenever Maxwell Hartley publishes a new book. There's no charge and no obligation.

https://books2read.com/r/B-A-LOJZ-OKLLC

BOOKS 2 READ

Connecting independent readers to independent writers.

About the Author

Maxwell Hartley is a relationship coach, author, and advocate for authentic connections. With a deep passion for helping individuals build and sustain meaningful relationships, Maxwell has dedicated his career to guiding others on their journey towards love and connection.

Drawing from his own experiences and extensive research in psychology and communication, Maxwell offers practical insights and actionable advice in his writing. His warm and empathetic approach resonates with readers, as he shares his wisdom on topics such as authenticity, emotional intimacy, and effective communication.

Maxwell's work is driven by a belief in the transformative power of genuine connections. He believes that when individuals embrace their true selves and foster deep connections based on trust and respect, they can create fulfilling and lasting relationships.

As a sought-after relationship coach, Maxwell has empowered countless individuals to navigate the complexities of love, overcome relationship challenges, and create harmonious connections. His coaching sessions and workshops have inspired personal growth, enriched communication skills, and provided individuals with the tools to cultivate love and happiness in their lives.

In addition to his coaching practice, Maxwell is an avid writer, sharing his insights and expertise through his books, articles, and online platforms. His relatable and accessible writing style makes complex concepts easily understandable, offering readers practical guidance to apply in their own lives.

Maxwell Hartley's mission is to inspire and empower individuals to build authentic and fulfilling relationships. Through his work, he continues to make a positive impact on the lives of individuals seeking genuine connections and love that stands the test of time.